PILOT's BASICS

EASY TO USE RULES OF THUMB,
FORMULAE AND FACTORS
FOR EVERY PILOT

Gerhard Grohmann

ISBN: 978-3-9501426-1-7

© Gerhard Grohmann – 4pilots

All rights reserved

4pilots
Gerhard Grohmann
6094 Axams, Austria, Europe
4pilots@speed.at

Many thanks to my friend and colleague
Captain Lane Hoy for his time.

Many thanks to my wife Dagmar,
for her help and understanding.

PILOT's BASICS

CONTENTS

Introduction		4
Chapter 1 **The Basics**		6
Chapter 2 **Mass, Area & Volume**		9
Chapter 3 **Distance & Speed**		12
Chapter 4 **Navigation**		18
Chapter 5 **Descent & Approach**		27
Chapter 6 **Other Calculations**		40
Chapter 7 **Time Calculations**		47
Chapter 8 **Quick Tips**		50
Chapter 9 **Summary of Formulae**		56
Chapter 10 **Abbreviations**		69
Chapter 11 **Tables**		71
Chapter 12 **Training Examples**		78
Chapter 13 **Checklist „Mnemonics**		84

PILOT's BASICS

INTRODUCTION

Thorough pre-flight preparation and planning is not, on its own, enough to perform a flight safely and at optimum efficiency.

Continuous reanalysis of our preparation, and adjustments to the plan to match the dynamic in-flight situation, is essential throughout any flight. This is a basic requirement, whether we are flying an Ultra-Light Aircraft, or on the flight deck of a modern Jumbo Jet.

During flight we continuously recalculate and estimate to confirm the accuracy of our pre-flight planning and calculations, or to fine tune them. For these re-calculations we often don't have another pilot, an FMS or even a calculator on hand to assist. Our heads and hands may be so busy that we just don't have the time for complex calculations.

In these situations rules of thumb, simple formulae and approximations are extremely helpful. A quick mental calculation or estimation will free us up for more pressing duties, thereby greatly improving overall safety.

"PILOT's BASICS" is a summary of Rules of Thumb and simple formulae commonly used in aviation – basic aviation knowledge – which will enable us to perform fast, simple and accurate mental calculations.

This book assists in developing and maintaining "Situational Awareness", the knowledge about our situation and position, which allow us to plan ahead easily and quickly. Rules Of Thumb therefore allow us to always stay "ahead of the aircraft", which in turn enables us to perform our duties efficiently and safely.

These rules and formulae result in close approximations of the normally required, but more complex, calculations. The results however are often not mathematically absolutely equal.

PILOT's BASICS

Therefore, these Rules Of Thumb should never be a substitute for mandated calculations in accordance with the relevant aviation regulations and standard operating procedures.

It is vital to correctly calculate and confirm critical values (such as remaining fuel, limiting crosswind components, and others) several times, by different means, to ensure that safety and legality is not in any way compromised.

Mental calculations, without any mechanical or electronic assistance, require learning and then constant practice, just as we had to learn and practice basic mathematics when in school. Only then we will be able to use the right formula to get the right result within the often brief time available to us.

But always remember the single most important Pilot's Rule of Thumb:

"Everything takes longer than planned"

Happy Landings!

Gerhard Grohmann

If you know of more or better Rules of Thumb and formulae, or if you have any comments or suggestions, please send me an email – let's try to improve "Pilot's Basics!"

4pilots@speed.at

PILOT's BASICS

CHAPTER 1

THE BASICS

It is vital to have a good understanding of, and be able to confidently use, basic mathematics when using any of these formulae for mental calculation.

Noting down important results - such as last fuel figures or estimated times - is an important safety issue: we may forget these results, or subsequently recall the wrong figure, and carry this forward into our next calculation.

To avoid making these errors, it is just good practice to note intermediate or final results, especially when busy, distracted or tired.

It is important to practice mental calculations in our daily lives (e.g. a discount of 15% when shopping, the average speed or the estimated time of arrival when driving our car).

Only with constant practice can we improve our mental calculation performance and accuracy.

a. Addition & Subtraction

We must be able to add and subtract 1 and 2 digit numbers (positive and negative) quickly and reliably.

> **Example:**
> - flight in FL 190,
> - outside air temperature –30°C
>
> What is the International Standard Temperature (ISA) at FL 190?
> What is the temperature difference between the actual and ISA?
>
> ⇨ ISA = (190 ÷ 10) x 2 = 38 subtract from 15° C – 38° C = –23°C
> ⇨ difference: –30° – 23° = 7°C colder than ISA

PILOT's BASICS

b. Multiplication & Division

In daily practice we only use multiples or divisions of a few numbers.

In most of cases, it is simply the multiples of 2 and 3 which affect our aircraft, e.g. the miles we fly per minute in climb, cruise and descent.

> **Example**:
> ✈ Descending through FL250, 80NM on the DME.
> Are we on the right descent profile?
> ⇨ (FL ÷ 10) x 3 + 10 = 85 NM
> ⇨ 85 NM – 80 NM = 5 NM
> ⇨ We are 5 NM too close, or 2000 FT too high!

As we have to do this calculation at least 5 times during the descent, this basic calculation must be fast and reliable. If our calculation takes too much time the result will no longer be relevant; any subsequent correction to the flight path will be inaccurate, as the basic figures of our calculation have changed.

c. Percentage Calculations & Fractions

3, 5, 10, 15, 20 and 25% are the most common percentages used, and we need to be particularly familiar with them. Much of the time exact results of percentage calculations are too detailed to have any practical effect, and it is also impractical to fly them.

Therefore we have to be familiar with rounding figures up and down, to keep our calculations simple and practical.

Fractions – $1/8$; $1/4$; $1/3$; $1/2$; $2/3$ – can be used directly or converted, if you are more familiar with this, into percentages ($1/8$ = 12.5%; $1/4$ = 25%; ½ = 50% etc.).

> **Example:**
> ✈ How many KTS are 360 KMH?
> ⇨ (360 ÷ 2) + 10 % = 180 + 18 = 198 KTS
> ⇨ sufficient is: 180 + 20 = 200 KTS

Whichever is easier to use in the actual situation should be applied.

PILOT's BASICS

d. Time-Speed-Distance Calculations

The conversion of hours, minutes and seconds into decimal figures, and vice versa, is a standard requirement for most of the Time-Speed-Distance calculations.

For this, we need to know the multiples and fractions of the numbers 3 and 6 by heart.

We must also always remember that 2.2 minutes is 2:12 (not 2 minutes and 20 seconds), and that 1:50 is definitely not the same as 1.5 hours.

e. Rounding & Reduction of Numbers:

All our Rules of Thumb need simple figures, so it is usual to round up or down, or to make reductions.

This can easily result in errors: we may be too generous or even completely wrong with the rounding or the reduction.

Therefore it is very important to know the principles of mathematic rounding and reduction, and when rounding off numbers to always be on the "safe" side.

And at the end of any calculation ask yourself: "Can this result be correct?"

> ✈ Mental arithmetic is easy, provided that you practice often.
> ✈ At the end of any calculation always ask yourself "Can this result be correct?"
> ✈ When you are tired, distracted or during a high workload situation, use a scratch pad and note your intermediate and final results.
> ✈ Note any result which is critical or you may need later, e.g. fuel status to divert (BINGO Fuel).

PILOT's BASICS

CHAPTER 2

MASSES, AREAS & VOLUMES

Calculating fuel figures is often tricky: The fuel quantity and weight is given in Gallons (British or US?), Pounds, Litres, Kilos, or Tons (metric or US?).

The fuel consumption is in Pounds, Kilo per Km, NM, or H, or whatever was used at the time of certification of the aircraft and approved by the Authority.

Fuel is sold is Europe in Litres and Tons, in other countries in Gallons, Pounds and Tons.

The quantity in Litres and Gallons has a variable relation to the weight, depending on the actual specific gravity, which varies with temperature.

As pre-flight calculations have to be as precise as possible the exact values must be used.

For checks during the progress of the flight it is acceptable to use Rules of Thumb formulae, as they are rounded up and will give a more conservative result than any precise calculation.

Use of the following tables:

100 LBS = 100 x 0.4536 = 45.36 KG

100 KG = 100 x 2.2045855 = 220.45855 LBS

a. **Masses**

MASSES – EXACT					
Mass	X	=	X	Mass
LBS	0.4536	KG	2.2045	LBS
KG	2.2045	LBS	0.4526	KG

MASSES – APPROXIMATION				
Mass	X	=	X	Mass
LBS	0.45	KG	2.2	LBS
(KG x 2) + 10% = LBS			(LBS ÷ 2) - 10% = KG	

9

PILOT's BASICS

b. Areas

AREAS – EXACT				
Area	X	=	X	Area
SQUARE FEET	0.0929	M²	10.764	SQUARE FEET

AREAS – APPROXIMATION				
Area	X	=	X	Area
SQUARE FEET	0.1	M²	11	SQUARE FEET

c. Volumes

VOLUMES – EXACT				
Volume	X	=	X	Volume
LITRE	0.2641	USG	3.7853	LITRE
IMPG	1.201	USG	0.8327	IMPG
IMPG	4.546	LITRE	0.2199	IMPG

VOLUMES – APPROXIMATION				
Volume	X	=	X	Volume
LITRE	**0.25**	**USG**	**3.8**	**LITRE**
IMPG	**1.2**	**USG**	**0.8**	**IMPG**
IMPG	**4.5**	**LITRE**	**0.2**	**IMPG**

AVGAS – EXACT				
Volume	X	Weight	X	Volume
LITRE	0.719		1.39	LITRE
USG	2.75	KG	0.3672	USG
IMPG	3.27		0.3058	IMPG
LITRE	1.58		0.631	LITRE
USG	6.00	LBS	0.167	USG
IMPG	7.18		0.1391	IMPG

PILOT's BASICS

Volume	X	Weight	X	Volume
LITRE	0.8		1.5	LITRE
USG	2.8	KG	0.4	USG
IMPG	3.3		0.3	IMPG
LITRE	1.6		0.6	LITRE
USG	6.0	LBS	0.2	USG
LITRE	7.2		0.15	IMPG

AVGAS – APPROXIMATION				
JET-FUEL – EXACT (JET A1, 15° C)				
Volume	X	Weight	X	Volume
LITRE	0.796		1.2565	LITRE
USG	3.085	KG	0.3241	USG
IMPG	3,618		0.2764	IMPG
LITRE	1.7547		0.57	LITRE
USG	6.7	LBS	0.1506	USG
IMPG	7,977		0.1254	IMPG

JET-FUEL – APPROXIMATION				
Volume	X	Weight	X	Volume
LITRE	0.8		1.25	LITRE
USG	3.0	KG	0.3	USG
IMPG	3.6		0.3	IMPG
LITRE	1.8		0.6	LITRE
USG	6.7	LBS	0.15	USG
IMPG	8.0		0.15	IMPG

PILOT's BASICS

CHAPTER 3

DISTANCES & SPEEDS

The sometimes confusing mix of different units for values of visibility and distance, such as Kilometres, Meters, Feet, Nautical or Statue Miles often requires a quick conversion within a short time.

This situation is compounded for flights within the metric system.

a. Distances

EXACT			APPROXIMATION
SM	KM	NM	(KM ÷ 2) + 10% = NM
0.6213	1	0.5399	(NM x 2) – 10% = KM
KM	NM	SM	(KM ÷ 2) + 20% = SM
1.852	1	1.1508	(SM x 2) – 20% = KM
KM	SM	NM	SM - 15% = NM
1.6096	1	0.8689	NM + 15% = SM
M	KM	FT	(FT ÷ 3) – 5% = KM
1.000	1	3208	(M x 3) + 5% = FT
M	NM	FT	FT ÷ 6000 = NM
1852	1	6076	NM x 6000 = FT
M	SM	FT	(FT ÷ 5000) – 5% = SM
1609	1	5280	(SM x 5000) + 5% = FT

PILOT's BASICS

b. Speeds

EXACT	
MPS*	FPM
1	196.85
5.08	1000
MPS	KTS
1	1.9438
0.5145	1
MPS	KMH**
1	3.6
0.277	1
KTS	KMH
1	1.852
0.53996	1

APPROXIMATION
(MPS x 100) x 2 = FPM
(FPM ÷ 100) ÷ 2 = MPS
MPS x 2 = KTS
½ KTS = MPS
(MPS x 3) + 20% = KMH
(KMH ÷ 3) − 20% = MPS
(KTS x 2) - 10% = KMH
(KMH ÷ 2) + 10% = KTS
Mach x 570 = KTAS

* MPS = Meter per Second

** KMH = Kilometres per Hour

c. RVR-Values

EXACT		
FEET	METER	SM
6000	1870	1¼
5000	1600	1
4000	1250	3/4
2400	750	1/2
1600	500	1/4
800	250	1/8
400	125	

APPROXIMATION		
METER	FACTOR	FT
1850 x 3 +	300 =	6000
1600 x 3 +	250 =	5000
1250 x 3 +	200 =	4000
750 x 3 +	150 =	2400
500 x 3 +	100 =	1600
250 x 3 +	50 =	800
125 x 3 +	25 =	400

PILOT's BASICS

d. Time-Speed-Distance (TSD)

The speed and distance an aircraft is flying within a certain period or phase of a flight is one of the most important values for any planning.

> **The basics:**
>
> **At a speed of 60 KTS an aircraft flies 1 NM distance in 1 MIN. All further values are multiples of this basic value.**

It is recommended that you memorise the following table, at least up to the maximum speed of your aircraft.

GROUND SPEED (KTS)	NM PER MINUTE (NM/MIN)
90	1.5
120	2.0
150	2.5
180	3.0
210	3.5
240	4.0
270	4.5
300	5.0
330	5.5
360	6.0
390	6.5
420	7.0
450	7.5
480	8.0

The basic formula for all TSD calculations is:

> **DISTANCE = GS x TIME**

Note that you have to add or deduct the actual wind component to/from your TAS (True Air Speed) to get your exact GS (Ground Speed).

PILOT's BASICS

During any flight we have to do numerous TSD calculations:

> **Example:**
> ✈ We shall descent from FL 310 to FL 130 with our normal ROD (Rate of Descent) of 3000 FPM (Feet per Minute) with an actual GS of 480 KTS.
>
> What distance will we have flown upon reaching FL 130?
> ⇨ with a GS of 480 KTS we will fly 8 NM/MIN
> ⇨ the total altitude we will descent is: 31000 – 13000 = 18000 FT
> ⇨ time required to descent through 18000 FT with a ROD of 3000 FT: 18000 ÷ 3000 = 6 MIN

For Mach values use the following formula:

$$M \times 10 = NM/MIN$$

> **Example:**
> ✈ M 0,8 x 10 = 8,0 NM/MIN

e. Equal Time point (ETP) – Distance

The ETP-D defines the point in NM on a route, where the flight time to the destination is equal to the flight time to the departure point.

$$\text{ETP-D} = \frac{\text{Total Distance} \times \text{Return Groundspeed (GS)}}{\text{Continue GS} + \text{Return GS}}$$

Continue GS is the ground speed when continuing the flight, Return GS is the groundspeed when returning to the departure point.

PILOT's BASICS

> **Example:**
> ✈ Total fuel on board: 5 hrs
> ✈ Total distance: 300 NM
> ✈ True airspeed: 100 KTS
> ✈ Headwind: 20 KTS
>   ⇨ ETP = (300 x 120) ÷ (80 + 120) = 36000 ÷ 200 = 180 NM
>
> The ETP-D is 180 NM apart from the departure point.

f. Equal Time Point (ETP) – Time

The ETP-T defines the point in time on a route, where the flight time to the destination is equal to the flight time to the departure point.

$$\text{ETP-T} = \text{ETP-D} \div \text{Continue GS}$$

> **Example:**
> ✈ ETP-D: 180 NM
> ✈ Continue GS: 80 KTS
>   ⇨ ETP = 180 ÷ 80 = 2,25 HRS = 2:15 HRS
>
> The ETP-T is 2:15 HRS apart from the departure point.

g. Point of No Return (PNR) – Distance

The PNR-D defines the point on a flight route in NM, after that a return to the departure point is impossible due to the fuel status.

$$\text{PRN-D} = \frac{\text{END} \times \text{GS} \times \text{Return GS}}{\text{Continue GS} + \text{Return GS}}$$

END = Endurance

PILOT's BASICS

> **Example:**
> ✈ Total fuel on board: 5 hrs
> ✈ True airspeed: 100 KTS
> ✈ Headwind: 20 KTS
>   ⇨ PRN-D = 5 x (80 x 120) / (80 + 120) = 5 x 9600/200 = 5 x 48 = 240 NM
>
> The PNR-D is 240 NM apart from the departure point.

h. Point of No Return (PNR) – Time

The PNR-T defines the point on a flight route in time, after that a return to the departure point is impossible due to the fuel status.

$$\text{PNR-T} = \text{PNR-D} \div \text{Continue GS}$$

> **Example:**
> ✈ PNR-D: 240 NM
> ✈ Continue GS: 80 KTS
>   ⇨ PNR-T = 240 ÷ 80 = 3,0 HRS = 3:00 HRS
>
> The PRN-T is 3:00 HRS apart from the departure point.

PILOT's BASICS

CHAPTER 4

NAVIGATION

a. Reciprocal Courses

Finding the reciprocal course can be done visually or arithmetically. In an older or simple aircraft cockpit we can read the reciprocal course directly from the compass.

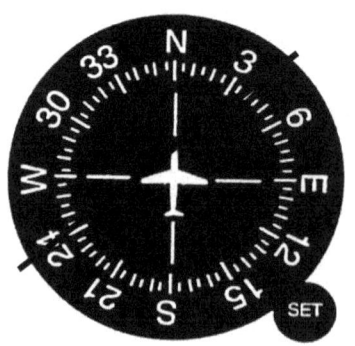

But to get the correct result we have to train the correct visual reading of the reciprocal course.

One of the requirements for a visual reading is that the entire compass rose is visible.

As this is not always the case in a modern glass cockpit, a mental calculation is required.

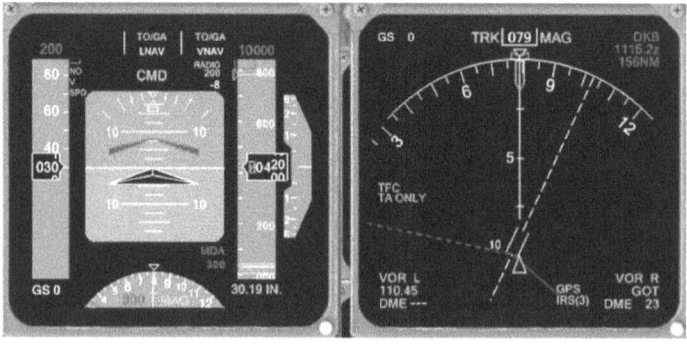

18

PILOT's BASICS

Without a compass rose it is quite complicated to add or subtract the 180° – it is easier to use this formula:

COURSE <180°:   RECIPROCAL COURSE = COURSE + 200° – 20°
COURSE >180°:   RECIPROCAL COURSE = COURSE – 200° + 20°

Example:
✈ 090° + 200° – 20° = 270°
✈ 146° + 200° – 20° = 326°
✈ 292° – 200° + 20° = 112°
The last figure always remains unchanged.

Alternative formula:

```
       COURSE =       0 0 0
                     +/–  2
                     –/+    2
RECIPROCAL COURSE =   X X X
```

The rules:
✈ The first sign +/– is depending on the start course.
✈ The first result must not be negative; the first figure must not be higher than 3.
✈ The second calculation must use the opposite sign of the first calculation.
✈ The last figure always remains unchanged.

Example:

✈ We are looking for the reciprocal course of 146°.
- as the last digit remains the same, we can forget it for the moment
  - left is the number 14
- as the course is smaller than 180° and as we don't want to have negative results, we add 2 to the first digit
  - 1 + 2 = 3
- And we do the contrary with the second digit by subtracting 2
  - 4 – 2 = 2
- now we have as the first digit 3 and as the second digit 2
  - this is the number 32
- now we remember the last digit of the start course and put this number to the end of our new number
  - 32 and 6 = 326° = the reciprocal course of 146°

Unfortunately this formula doesn't work with all courses; here we have to be flexible and to do either our math over the 360° mark, visualize the compass rose or use the +/-200 and +/-20 method.

COURSE	RECIPROCAL COURSE
167	347
255	075
003	183
222	042
328	148

PILOT's BASICS

b. DME-Arc – Intercept – "1 in 60" Rule

The "1 in 60" Rule uses the fact that at a distance of 60 NM from a VOR the distance between VOR radials is 1 NM.

This distance decreases linearly with the distance.

DME DISTANCE	1 DEGREE = NM
60	1
30	1/2 or 0.50
20	1/3 or 0.33
15	1/4 or 0.25
12	1/5 or 0.20
10	1/6 or 0.16

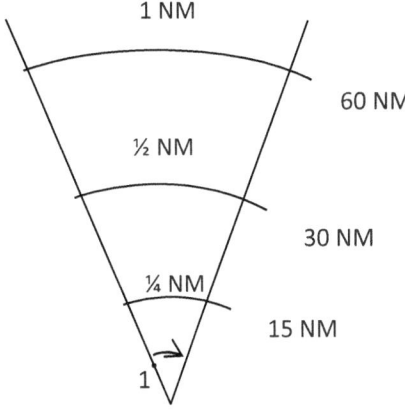

When planning for a DME-ARC approach we can use this linear reduction to our advantage.

PILOT's BASICS

> **Example:**
> ✈ We are approaching a VOR on the radial 047 and have to fly on a 16 DME-arc to the radial 011.
>
> How long is the DME arc?
>
> ⇨ calculate the number of crossing radials
>
> 047 – 011 = 36 radials
>
> ⇨ calculate the numbers of radials per NM
>
> In a distance of 16 NM the distance between 2 radials is approximately ¼ NM
>
> ⇨ 36 radials x ¼ NM = 9 NM

To enable us to do this calculation mentally, we have to use an approximation of known numbers.

Therefore, even if we are on a 16 or 14 DME-arc, as in this example, we use the closest known number for our calculation – in this case 15 NM/ ¼ NM.

We need to remember the values for the above distances over a longer period. Then using the closest number makes no real difference in practical flying.

c. Flight Time on a DME-Arc

Now, it is easy to calculate the flight time on this DME-arc at the planned speed.

> **Example:**
> ✈ 180 KTAS, DME-Arc = 9 NM
> ⇨ with 180 KTS we fly 3 NM/MIN = 3 MIN for 9 NM

d. Turn Radius – "Lead Point" on a DME-Arc

Another task when flying on a DME-Arc is to determine the "Lead Point" or the "Lead Radial". This is the point where we start to turn on to the inbound radial or the localizer.

PILOT's BASICS

To calculate this, we have to know the distance flown in a turn. This distance or turn radius depends on the actual speed and bank angle.

For a Standard Rate Turn (SRT) – 3° per second – we can use 2 formulae for the low speed range:

> **TURN RADIUS (NM) = TAS ÷ 200**

or

> **TURN RADIUS (NM) = (TAS x 1%) ÷ 2**

In the high speed range (from 200 KTS or M0.4 upwards) and when using a 30° bank angle we have to use the Mach formula:

> **TURN RADIUS (NM) = (MACH NUMBER x 10) – 2**

> **Example:**
> ✈ 200 KTAS, Standard Rate Turn
>   ⇨ 200 ÷ 200 = 1 NM or (200 x 1%) = 2 ÷ 2 = 1 NM
> For our 16 NM DME-arc we will have the following Lead Radial:
>   ⇨ distance between radials at 16 NM = ¼ NM
>   ⇨ 1 NM ÷ ¼ NM = 4 radials
>   ⇨ 4 radials before the inbound or localizer course at the latest we should turn with a SRT on to the inbound course
> For our example we should set the radial 011 + 4 = R015 and should have our Standard Rate Turn (SRT) when the radial is centred on our VOR indicator.

e. Standard Rate Turn (SRT)

The next question will be, which Bank Angle has to be flown at a certain speed to get the SRT or Rate One Turn.

PILOT's BASICS

BANK ANGLE (SRT) = (TAS ÷ 10) x 1.5

or

BANK ANGLE (SRT) = (TAS + (TAS ÷ 2)) ÷ 10

or

BANK ANGLE (SRT) = (TAS ÷ 10) + 7

Example:
✈ 180 KTAS
 ⇨ (180 ÷ 10) x 1.5 = 18 x 1.5 = 27°
 ⇨ (180 + (180 ÷ 2)) ÷ 10 = (180 + 90) ÷ 10 = 270 ÷ 10 = 27°
 ⇨ (180 ÷ 10) + 7 = 18 + 7 = 25°
 ⇨ 15% von 180 = 27°

KTAS	SRT – BANK ANGLE	TURN RADIUS (NM)
90	13.5°	0.5
120	18°	0.6
200	30°	1
M 0.80	30°	6

f. Base Turn Angle (BT-Angle)

Some approaches require flying a Base Turn (BT) procedure. With this formula we can calculate the correct opening angle and also the correct outbound time.

This enables us to minimize later corrections when turning on to the inbound course.

BT-ANGLE = <u>FACTOR 36 (54)</u>
OUTBOUND TIME

use factor 36 up to 170 KTS
use factor 54 above 170 KTS

PILOT's BASICS

> OUTBOUND TIME = <u>FACTOR 36 (54)</u>
> BT-ANGLE
>
> use factor 36 up to 170 KTS
> use factor 54 above 170 KTS

g. Magnetic Compass Turns

When flying turns only with the magnetic compass in the northern hemisphere we have to know the following rules:

✈ When turning on to a northerly heading the indication of the magnetic compass lags behind. The turn has to be finished before the compass indicates the new heading.

✈ When turning on to a southerly heading the indication of the magnetic compass leads ahead. The turn has to be finished after the compass indicates the new heading.

✈ The amount of lead and lag is at the highest on north-south headings and depends on the actual bank angle in the turn and the latitude of the position of the aircraft.

Remember:

> UNOS – Undershoot North, Overshoot South

On easterly and westerly courses a magnetic compass deviates
⇨ during an acceleration to the north
⇨ during a deceleration to the south

Remember:

> ANDS – Accelerate North, Decelerate South

PILOT's BASICS

h. "Lead-Point" for "Magnetic" Turns

The turn has to be stopped at that indication of the magnetic compass, at which the following value has been added or subtracted from the planned heading.

> **Latitude +/- 1/3 of the Bank Angle (BA)**

> **LP = TARGET COURSE +/- (LAT +/- 1/3 BA)**

Example:
- bank angle: 15° thereof $1/3 = 5°$
- start-heading: 270°
- target-heading: 360°
- latitude: 45° N
  ⇨ Lead Point: 360 – (45 + 5) = 360 - 50 = 310°

(accelerate NORTH, therefore +)

- bank angle: 15° thereof $1/3 = 5°$
- start-heading: 270°
- target-heading: 180°
- latitude: 30° N
  ⇨ Lead Point: 180 – (30 - 5) = 180 - 25 = 155°

(decelerate SOUTH, therefore -)

BANK ANGLE	START HEADING	TARGET HEADING	LATITUDE	LEAD POINT
15°	270°	360°	30° N	325°
15°	270°	180°	30° N	155°
25°	090°	010°	40° N	058°
25°	090°	190°	40° N	222°
15°	270°	360°	45° N	320°
15°	270°	180°	34° N	151°
25°	360°	090°	40° N	082°
20°	090°	190°	40° N	223°

PILOT's BASICS

CHAPTER 5

CLIMB, DESCENT & APPROACH

a. Minimum Climb Gradient

Many standard departures and missed approaches require a Minimum Climb Gradient to ensure terrain clearance and/or minimum noise.

This Minimum Climb Gradient is given either in % or in feet per NM (FT/NM).

As the Required Climb Rates in FPM at a certain speed are not always given, here is the formula:

% x GS = ROC/ROD in FPM

or

FT/NM x (GS ÷ 60)

or

% x Mach x 1.000 = ROC/ROD in FPM

Example:
- ✈ Required Climb Gradient: 3.0%
- ✈ GS = 150 KTS
    - ⇨ 3.0 x 150 = 450 FPM
- ✈ Minimum Required Climb Gradient: 3,0%
- ✈ M = 0,7
    - ⇨ 3.0 x 0.6 x 1000 = 1800 FPM

PILOT's BASICS

b. Descent

There are 3 basic methods for descent planning:
- ✈ "3 in 1" Method
- ✈ Constant Sink Rate
- ✈ Pitch Attitude

"3 in 1" Method

Jets normally use this method, as their descent is performed with idle power.

(ACTUAL FL – PLANNED FL) ÷ 10 x 3+10 = DIST (NM)

+

+/– 2 NM for each 10 KTS Head- or Tailwind

---

or

(ACTUAL FL – PLANNED FL) ÷ 3 + 10 = DIST (NM)

+

+/– 2 NM for each 10 KTS Head- or Tailwind

The result is the distance from the point, at which we want to have reached the planned altitude.

- ✈ If we can't or don't want to use speed brakes or the gear to reduce the speed at lower altitudes, we will not be able to keep up the descent rate. Therefore the distance needs to be increased by 10 NM.
- ✈ Any head- or tailwind has a large influence on distance flown and on planned altitude. With a headwind we have to reduce the distance by 2 NM per 10 KTS wind, with a tailwind to increase by 2 NM per 10 KTS wind.
- ✈ The two formulae will give slightly different sink rates (300 and 333 FT/NM). The second formula results in a 10% greater distance and is the more conservative for descent planning.

Constant Sink Rate

This method is used for turboprops and fast piston engine aircraft, which are looking for a constant sink rate at a constant GS. There is no straight formula available, but we can use a combination of the different calculations.

> **Example:**
> ✈ Out of FL 230 we must reach FL 110 at the VOR ABC. GS is 240 KTS, the constant sink rate is 2000 FPM.
>
> When do we have to start the descent?
> ⇨ Altitude to descent: 23000 – 11000 = 12000 FT
> ⇨ Descent time: 12000 ÷ 2000 = 6 MIN = 4 NM/MIN
> ⇨ Total distance: 4 x 6 = 24 NM before VOR ABC

Pitch Attitude Descent

This method is used mostly in general aviation, with single engine aircraft and also during the (basic) IFR training. It seems to be complicated, but it isn't – have a look!

To ensure the correct pitch attitude change, we assume a 0-pitch indication on our artificial horizon.

We further assume that there will be no changes in the pitch due to a change in the aircraft configuration (by setting flaps or extending the gear). The power will be set to keep a constant speed during the descent.

PILOT's BASICS

> **Example:**
> ✈ Flight at FL 130, GS of 120 KTAS
> ✈ Clearance: Descent to FL030 within 30 NM
>
> For this method we do need to know the altitude to descent and the distance within we have to descent to this altitude.
>
> ⇨ Distance to descent is 30 NM.
> ⇨ Mentally we now place this 30 NM on the 10° nose-down line on our horizon and divide the area between the 0° line and the 10° line into 30 lines.
> ⇨ Altitude to descent (in FL): 130 – 30 = 10 FL
> ⇨ Now we put the number 10 on the 10th line of our 30 lines.
> ⇨ 10 is $1/3$ of 30, therefore our target attitude is $1/3$ of the 10° pitch attitude, which is 3.3° nose down.

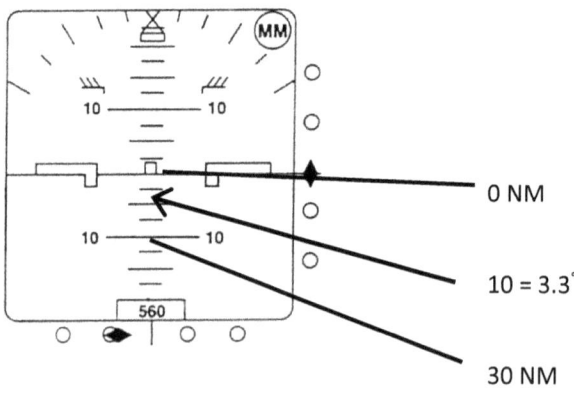

PILOT's BASICS

b. Correction of Altitude Deviations

During climbs, descents or an approach, or when correcting small altitude deviations in the cruise, this formula calculate the correct adjustment in advance:

> **ROD/ROC (FPM) = DEVIATION x 2**
> **ROD = Rate of Descent in FPM**
> **ROC = Rate of Climb in FPM**

> **Example:**
> ✈ deviation 200 FT =>
>   ⇨ correct using 400 FPM

c. Level Off

To achieve a smooth level of at the assigned or planned altitude adjust your Rate of Descent (ROD) or Rate of Climb (ROC) using the following formula:

> **ROD/ROC within 1000 FT = ALTITUDE TO GO**

> **Example:**
> ✈ 700 FT above/below the assigned/planned altitude
>   ⇨ ROD/ROC = 700 FPM
> ✈ 300 FT above/below the assigned/planned altitude
>   ⇨ ROD/ROC = max 300 FPM

d. Wind Corrections

For all descents and approaches we have to take the actual wind into consideration. The wind may have a remarkable influence to our GS, especially at higher altitudes, and will affect all our calculations.

PILOT's BASICS

But calculating effects of the wind shouldn't be too complicated and should not require another TSD-calculation, as we have to do these calculations anyway during every descent and approach.

For most aircraft the value of 1.65 NM, rounded up to 2 NM per 10 KTS wind has been proven to be accurate and easy to use. Therefore we are using this value in the "3 to 1 Method"

Explanation:

An aircraft needs approximately 10 minutes from the Top of Descent (TOD) to the initial altitude for the approach.

A jet descents with approximately 3000 FPM out of FL 350, a turboprop with approximately 2000 FPM out of FL 250 and a single engine aircraft with approximately 1000 FPM to start the approach at between 3000 and 5000 FT above the airport elevation.

At a speed of 60 KTS an aircraft flies 1 NM/MIN, therefore in 10 MIN:

- ⇨ 10.0 NM at 60 KTAS
- ⇨ 5.0 NM at 30 KTAS
- ⇨ 2.5 NM at 15 KTAS
- ⇨ 1.65 NM at 10 KTAS

These are the distances an aircraft will be moved by an equivalent wind plus/minus the own speed.

But it has to be noted that for an aircraft at 120 KTAS a wind of 30 KTS is 25% of its own speed, but it is only 6% of the total speed for an aircraft flying with 480 KTAS.

These relations have the same notable influence on all wind related TSD-calculations.

PILOT's BASICS

Crosswind (XWind)

With the take-off or landing clearance we get the latest wind from the tower. If this wind is quite strong from an inconvenient direction we have to be able to calculate fast, if wind speed and direction are within the limits.

✈ To calculate the correct wind factor and the correct XWind, we first have to know the angle between the runway (RWY) and the wind direction.

It is not important if the wind is from the left or right.

✈ On the runway and on final we can easily read this wind angle from the compass rose.

Even in a glass cockpit the reduced compass rose should be wide enough. However, if not, even more attention should be given to the actual wind situation, as the wind might be very strong or even too strong for take-off or landing.

Runway Direction

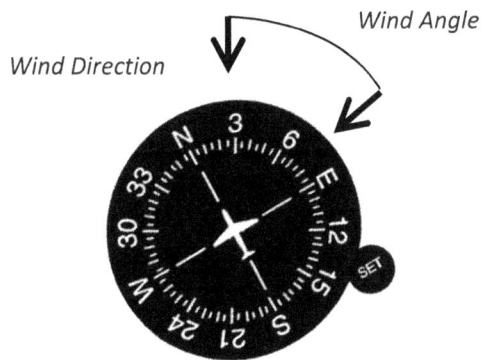

Wind Angle

Wind Direction

✈ We should know the following table by heart: Knowing the wind angle, we look for the closest value and the according factor.

WIND ANGLE	FACTOR	XWIND-FACTOR	XWIND-COMPONENT
000°	0.0	0 %	nothing
030°	0.5	50 %	half
045°	0.7	70 %	2/3
060°	0.9	90 %	nearly full
090°	1.0	100 %	full

PILOT's BASICS

This table is mathematically not exact, but it is good enough for a quick evaluation shortly before take-off or landing.

> **Example:**
> ✈ approach to RWY 03, wind 080/40
>   ⇨ wind angle: 50°
>   ⇨ closest wind angle in the table is 045°, so we use the factor 0.7
>   ⇨ 40 KTS x 0.7 = 28 KTS XWind, in this case from the right.
>
> If the wind was 310/40, we do the same calculation and will get the same result – except that the wind is now from the other side, from the left.

When evaluating the take-off and landing situation in the flight planning, it is important to remember, that wind reported in METARs and TAFs is true wind.

The actual wind angle - the difference to the runway direction, which is always in magnetic - might be considerable at airports with a large variation.

However, the actual wind as reported by the tower is always magnetic wind.

WIND ANGLE	WIND SPEED	XWIND
030°	20	10
050°	20	14
070°	18	16

e. Drift Corrections

To fly an approach with a known drift correction is much easier than trying to work out the drift during the approach when the workload is high.

For cruise and the approach we can use the following formula:

> **DRIFT CORRECTION = (XWIND COMPONENT x 60) ÷ TAS**

PILOT's BASICS

Note that this formula becomes less accurate with strong XWinds and corresponding high drift corrections (over 15°).

Example:
- ✈ approach with 120 KTAS, 20 KTS XWind component
  - ⇨ (20 x 60) ÷ 120 = 1200 ÷ 120 = 10°
- ✈ cruise with 400 KTAS, 80 KTS XWind component
  - ⇨ (80 x 60) ÷ 420 = 4800 ÷ 400 = 12°

Or use one of these formulae for your calculations:

DRIFT CORRECTION = XWIND COMPONENT ÷ Y
(Y = NM/MIN)

Example:
- ✈ cruise with 240 KTAS, 20 KTS XWind component
  - ⇨ 240 KTAS = 4 NM/MIN
  - ⇨ 20 ÷ 4 = 5°

DRIFT CORRECTION = (WIND ANGLE x WIND SPEED) ÷ TAS

Example:
- ✈ runway 27, wind 300/12
  - ⇨ wind angle = 300 − 270 = 30
  - ⇨ 30 x wind speed = 30 x 12 = 360
  - ⇨ drift correction = 360 ÷ TAS = 360 ÷ 100 = 3.6°

PILOT's BASICS

When flying Mach numbers:

Take a 1° drift correction for each knot of XWind component, which is 10 times the actual Mach number.

1° DRIFT CORRECTION = XWIND COMPONENT ÷ (M x 10)

Example:
- M 0.80, XWind 48 KTS
  - 48 ÷ (0.80 x 10) = 48 ÷ 8 = 6° drift

TAS	XWIND	DRIFT CORRECTION
150	12	4.8
360	48	8
90	30	20
M 0.78	50	6.4

f. Course Corrections

Small calculated corrections to any deviations during the approach, or when tracking a radial, are much more successful than fast and exaggerated reactions.

This formula should be used to determine the required bank angle for all corrections. The maximum bank angle of 30° or 3° per second should never be exceeded.

BANK ANGLE = HEADING TO GO

Example:
- VOR-Tracking, 2 dots deviation = 4° deviation
  - bank angle = 4°

g. Visual Descent Point (VDP)

The VDP is defined as the point during a non-precision approach at which a descent from the MDA may be commenced, provided the required visibility is available.

But even for a VFR approach it is quite helpful to define a VDP, as this will ensure a constant, controlled and stable descent to the RUNWAY.

The VDP should be defined early enough before commencing the final descent, as later corrections have proven not to be very successful.

The VDP ensures a normal 3° slope to the runway, on the VASI, if available.

For a VOR or LOC approach a DME distance may define the VDP.

If there is no VDP defined on the approach plate, we have 2 simple methods to define this point.

Note that for both methods a higher or lower approach speed results in a shallower or steeper approach angle from the VDP to the runway. Therefore choosing and consequently flying a specific speed is important.

VDP-DME – Method

This method will result in a sink rate of approximately 300 FT/NM to the threshold, similar to a 3° glide slope.

As the name suggest, a DME or other reliable source, (such as a GPS) to measure the distance to the runway, is required.

$$\text{VDP (DME)} = \text{HAT} \div 300$$

Example:
- MDA = 2760 FT, RUNWAY elevation = 2368 FT
  - HAT = MDA – RUNWAY elevation = 392
  - 392 ÷ 300 = 1.31 NM = 1.3 NM

PILOT's BASICS

VDP – Timing – Method

Is there no DME or any other distance source available we can use the time to define the VDP.

> **VDP (SEC) = HAT ÷ 10**

Explanation:

Dividing the Height Above Threshold (HAT) by 10 results in a sink rate of 10 FT/SEC, which is 600 FPM.

This formula gives us the time in seconds from the Minimum Descent Altitude (MDA) to the threshold with a sink rate of 600 FPM.

This time will now be deducted from the known and given time from the Final Approach Fix (FAF) to the Missed Approach Point (MAP).

> **Example:**
> ✈ HAT = 392 FT
> ✈ time FAF – MAP (with 120 KTS) = 2:15 MIN
>   ⇨ 392 ÷ 10 = 39.2 SEC
>   ⇨ 2:15 – 0:39 = 1:36 MIN   FAF → VDP

Any higher or slower approach speed can be accepted, as the difference is ignorable. However, the right time has to be taken in accordance with the planned GS.

> **Example:**
> ✈ HAT = 392 FT
> ✈ time FAF – MAP (160 KTS) = 1:42 MIN
>   ⇨ 392 ÷ 10 = 39.2 SEC
>   ⇨ 1:42 – 0:39 = 1:03 MIN   FAF → VDP

h. Descent Rate

With this formula we can calculate the required descent rate early enough.

On a 3° glide path the descent rate depends only from the GS the aircraft is flying.

However, to reach the MAP on a Non Precision Approach in time, it is recommended to increase slightly the calculated descent rate, to be in time at the MDA.

> **ROD (FPM) = GS x 5**
>
> (+ 200 FPM at Non Precision Approaches)

> **Example:**
>
> ✈ approach with 3° GP, GS = 120 KTS
>
> ⇨ ROD = 120 x 5 = 600 FPM (Precision Approaches)
>
> at Non Precision Approaches:
>
> + 200 FPM = 800 FPM

PILOT's BASICS

CHAPTER 6

OTHER CALCULATIONS

a. True Airspeed (TAS)

The formula to calculate TAS is:

$$KTAS = KIAS + [(KIAS \times (ALT \text{ in } 1000s)) \times 2\%]$$

KIAS	ALTITUDE	KTAS
100	10000	120
140	5000	154
280	FL 350	476

An alternative formula:

$$TAS = IAS + Z\%$$

$Z\% = 2 \times ALT$ (in 1000 ft)

> **Example:**
> ✈ IAS = 120 KTS, altitude = 15000 FT
>   ⇨ TAS = 120 x Z%
>   ⇨ Z = 2 x 15 = 30%
>   ⇨ 30% of 120 = 36 KTS
>   ⇨ TAS = 120 + 36 = 156 KTAS

PILOT's BASICS

b. Temperatures

There are 3 easy and quick formulae available to convert Celsius (C) in Fahrenheit (F), and vice versa.

The easiest unfortunately has the disadvantage of being slightly inaccurate in the higher temperature range:

$$°F = (2 \times °C) + 30$$
$$°C = (°F - 30) \div 2$$

These 2 formulae are more accurate, but do need some extra calculation:

$$°F = (2 \times °C) - 10\% + 32$$
$$°C = [(°F - 32) + 10\%] \div 2$$

or

$$°F = (9/5 \times °C) + 32$$
$$°C = (°F - 32) \times 5/9$$

A comparison between the formulae, showing their accuracy:

	CELSIUS => FAHRENHEIT		
°C	METHOD 1	METHOD 2	METHOD 3
12	(2 x 12) + 30 = 54	(2x12-2.4)+32=53.6	(12÷5x9)+32=53.6
25	(2 x 25) + 30 = 80	(2x25-5)+32=77	(25÷5x9)+32=77
0	(2 x 0) + 30 = 30	(2x0-0)+32=32	(0:5x9)+32=32

	FAHRENHEIT => CELSIUS		
°F	METHOD 1	METHOD 2	METHOD 3
40	(40 - 30) ÷ 2 = 5	((40-32)+0.8)÷2=4.4	(40-32)÷9x5=4.4
81	(81 - 30) ÷ 2 = 25.5	((81-32)+4.9)÷2=27	(81-32)÷9x5=27.2
72	(72 - 30) ÷ 2 = 21	((72-32)+4)÷2=22	(72-32)÷9x5=22.2

PILOT's BASICS

c. Standard Temperature (ISA)

The performance of our aircraft at any given altitude depends very much on the temperature at that altitude.

To decide whether to climb further or to stay at our present altitude we need to know the deviation from ISA.

ISA TEMPERATURE (°C) = 15 – (FL ÷ 10 x 2)

ALTITUDE	ISA TEMP	ACTUAL TEMP	TEMP DEVIATION
5000	5	20	+15
8000	-1	15	+16
FL 210	-27	-10	+17
FL 350	-49	-60	-11

d. Air Pressure

The Barometric Pressure changes with the altitude:

1 MB per ±30 FT

Conversion MB/HPA – INCH

1 INCH = 33.863 MB/HPA
1 MB/HPA = 0.02953 INCH

Pressure Altitude – PA

There are 2 methods to calculate the actual Pressure Altitude:

- Set the altimeter to 1013 MB/29.92 INCH and read the altitude = Pressure Altitude.
- Divide the difference between the indicated altitude at 1013 MB/29.92 INCH and the pressure indication of the altimeter at the field elevation by 30 and add or deduct it from the airport elevation.

PILOT's BASICS

> **PA = FE +/- [(1013 – ALT) ÷ 30]**
>
> Is the altimeter reading
>
> * above 1013 MB: deduct the correction from the field elevation
>
> * below 1013 MB: add the correction to the field elevation

> **Example:**
> ✈ airport elevation: 760 FT
> ✈ indicated altimeter reading: 1025 MB
>   ⇨ 1013 – 1025 = -12 MB
>   ⇨ -12 x 30 = -360 FT
>   ⇨ 760 – 360 = 400 FT Pressure Altitude

Density Altitude – DA

We need the Pressure Altitude to calculate the Density Altitude, which is required to calculate performance data.

The Density Altitude increases or decreases by 120 ft per each 1°C deviation of the actual Outside Air Temperature (OAT) from ISA.

> **DA = PA +/– 120 x D**
> **D = OAT – ISA**
>
> OAT warmer: add it to the PA
> OAT colder: deduct it from the PA

> **Example:**
> ✈ Pressure Alt = 6000 FT, OAT = 13°C, ISA = 3°C
>   ⇨ Density Altitude = 6000 + 120 x (13 – 3)
>   ⇨ 6000 + 1200 = 7200 FT DA

Temperature Correction of the Indicated Altitude

The correct indication of the Indicated Altitude depends on the actual temperature.

To calculate the True Altitude (TA) because of the deviation of the actual temperature from ISA add or deduct 4 FT for 1°C deviation from ISA for each 1000 FT.

TA CORRECTION = (OAT – ISA) x 4 FT per 1000 FT

Example:
- indicated altitude = 5000 FT, OAT = 0°C
- ISA in 5000 FT: 5°C
    - deviation: 0 – 5 = -5°C
    - 5000 FT x 4 FT = 20 FT
    - 20 x –5 = -100 FT
    - 5000 – 100 = 4900 FT

e. Cloud Base

If you know the ISA lapse rate of 2.5°C per 1.000FT, you can then calculate the Cloud Base.

This is very useful, particularly when you plan to fly over a mountain ridge or mountain pass and you do not have the actual local weather, but only the weather from an airport nearby.

The difference between the actual temperature and the dew point is called the Dew Point Spread.

CLOUD BASE = SPREAD (0C) x 400 (in FT)

or

CLOUD BASE = SPREAD (0C) : 2,5 (in 1.000 FT)

or

CLOUD BASE = SPREAD (0C) x 125 (in M)

PILOT's BASICS

f. Fuel Dumping

This is a simple calculation, as we always know 2 of 3 figures.

> **DUMP TIME = FUEL TO DUMP ÷ DUMP RATE**

> **FUEL TO DUMP = DUMP RATE x TIME**

But we may face one problem: Calculating with big numbers is quite tricky, and may lead to errors.

It is convenient then to use a simple reduction. By deleting the same amount of zeros from the end of each number we are using, the resulting numbers are quite easily handled.

> **Example:**
> ✈ 6500 ÷ 1300 = 65 ÷ 13 = 5

DUMP RATE	TIME	FUEL DUMPED
2500	18	45000
3000	6	18000
2000	10	20000

g. Hydroplaning Speed

It is important to know the Hydroplaning Speed of your aircraft for take-off and especially for landing.

The only information you need to calculate this speed is the tyre pressure in PSI and the following formula.

$$V_{HP}\,(\text{KTS}) = 9 \times \sqrt[2]{\text{TIRE PRESSURE (PSI)}}$$

45

PILOT's BASICS

As we won't know the square root or our tyre pressure from memory, we should pre-calculate the Hydroplaning Speed of our aircraft (and perhaps of our car also) occasionally in the comfort of our home, and then we can recall this instantly when required.

TYRE PRESSURE (PSI)	V_{HP} (KTS)
50	63
120	99
150	110 (rounded)
230	135 (rounded)

PILOT's BASICS

CHAPTER 7

TIME CALCULATIONS

a. Time in Decimals

The organization of our time system is unfortunately not in accordance with the decimal system, as we have 60 minutes per hour, 60 seconds per minute (however, in sports we are dividing the seconds in tenths and hundreds of seconds).

This doesn't make calculations easy, especially when we need the time in a formula within the decimal system.

MIN/SEC	DECIMAL	MIN/SEC	DECIMAL
3	0.05	33	0.55
6	0.10	36	0.60
9	0.15	39	0.65
12	0.20	42	0.70
15	0.25	45	0.75
18	0.30	48	0.80
21	0.35	51	0.85
24	0.40	54	0.90
27	0.45	57	0.95
30	0.50	60	1.00

It is therefore important to be accustomed to converting minutes and seconds into decimals – 1:30 h is not 1.3 h, but 1.5 h.

6 minutes is 0.1 h and the multiples thereof are the tenths of an hour. The same is valid for the seconds with a minute.

For more accurate conversions we can use 3 minutes, which is 0.05 h.

PILOT's BASICS

b. Addition/Subtraction of times

For many, the addition of flight times is quite a challenging and tiring job, and often results in errors. Worse still is subtraction of times.

Using the method below you can use any normal calculator; the job will be fast, simple and correct.

- ✈ All times are entered in your calculator like any other normal number, except that a zero is substituted for the colon between the hours and the minutes – e.g. 4:50 h will be entered as 4050.
- ✈ You can now do any addition and/or subtraction.
- ✈ When you are finished, you add the number 940 to the result as many times you need to see a zero at the third last digit <u>and</u> until the last 2 digits are not more than 59.

This may require multiple additions of 940, but sooner or later you will see the last 3 digits as required.

- ✈ To finish your calculation you now just substitute the third last digit, the zero, by a colon to get the result.
- ✈ The numbers before the colon are the hours, and behind the colon are the minutes.

<u>Example Addition</u>

TIME		INPUT INTO THE CALCULATOR
4:56	=	4056
2:18	=	+ 2018
1:55	=	+ 1055
5:20	=	+ 5020 =
14:29		12149 third last digit is not 0 ➔
		+ 940 =
		13089 the 2 last digits are above 59 ➔
		+ 940 =
		14029 ➔ 14:29 H

PILOT's BASICS

Example Subtraction

TIME		INPUT INTO THE CALCULATOR
14:07	=	14007
- 4:56	=	- 4056
- 2:18	=	- 2018
- 1:55	=	- 1055 =
4:58		6878 third last digit is not 0 ➔
		- 940 =
		5938 third last digit is not 0 ➔
		- 940 =
		4998 third last digit is not 0 ➔
		-940 =
		4058 ➔ 4:58 H

With this method we can also do any mixed time calculations, but before each change we have to first get a correct time indication.

Example mixed calculation

TIME		INPUT INTO THE CALCULATOR
14:07	=	14007
- 4:56	=	- 4056
9:11	=	9951 third last digit is not 0 ➔
		- 940 =
		9011 (= 9:11 H)
+1:55		+ 1055 =
11:06	=	10066 the 2 last digits are above 59 ➔
		+ 940 =
		11006 ➔ 11:06 H

49

PILOT's BASICS

CHAPTER 8

QUICK TIPS

Like all other Rules of Thumb these special Quick Tips are ONLY ESTIMATES for smaller aircrafts; these estimates shall never be a substitute for any required performance calculation.

Take Off & Climb

> Rotation Speed V_R is equal to approximately 1.15 x Stall Speed V_S.
>
> VR = VS x 1.15

> The Takeoff Distance increases 15% per 1000 FT Density Altitude above Sea Level (SL).
>
> + 1000 FT DA = TAKE OFF DISTANCE + 15%

> Any 1° C deviation of the Actual Temperature (OAT) from ISA will increase or decrease the Take Off Roll by 10%.
>
> +/-1°C ISA = TAKE OFF DISTANCE +/- 10%

> A Headwind of 10% of the Take Off Speed reduces the Ground Roll Distance by 10%.
>
> 10% H-WIND = GROUND ROLL DIST – 10%

> A Tailwind of 10% of the Take Off Speed increases the Ground Roll Distance by 20%.
>
> 10% T-WIND = GROUND ROLL DIST + 20%

> A Take Off should be rejected when 70% of the Take Off Speed is not reached within half the distance of Available Take Off Distance.

PILOT's BASICS

Soft ground can increase the Take Off Distance by 50%.

A 10% change of the Gross Weight changes the Take Off Distance by 20%.

+10% GW = TAKE OFF DISTANCE + 20%

Slush or wet snow can double the Take Off Distance or can make a Take Off impossible.

The loss of 1 engine in a 2-engined aircraft results in an 80% decrease of the Climb Rate.

The Best Rate of Climb Speed decreases by 1 KT per 1000 FT.

To get the Required Climb Gradient: Divide the height of the obstacle above the airport by the distance.

CLIMB GRADIENT (FPM) = ALTITUDE ÷ DISTANCE

Example:
- ✈ obstacle height: = 1000 FT, distance = 5 NM
- ✈ 1.000 ÷ 5 = 200 FPM Climb Gradient

To get the Required Climb Rate: Multiply the Climb Speed in FT/MIN by the Ground Speed expressed in NM/MIN.

REQUIRED CLIMB RATE = CLIMB SPEED X GS

Example:
- ✈ climb gradient = 200 FT/NM, GS = 120 KTS
- ✈ 120 ÷ 60 = 2 NM/MIN
- ✈ 2 x 200 = 400 FPM required Climb Rate

PILOT's BASICS

To get the Required Climb Rate: Multiply the Climb Gradient in % by the Ground Speed expressed in KTS.

REQUIRED CLIMB RATE = CLIMB GRADIENT X GS

Example:
- climb gradient = 3.3 %, GS = 120 KTS
- 3.3 x 120 = ~ 400 FPM

To get the Required Climb Rate in %: Divide the Obstacle Height in FT by 60 times the distance in NM.

REQUIRED CLIMB RATE = HEIGHT ÷ (60 x NM)

Example:
- obstacle height = 1000 FT, distance = 5 NM
- 1000 ÷ (60 x 5) = 3.3 %

To get the Required Climb Rate in % at a given speed: Divide the Required Climb Rate in FPM by the given Ground Speed expressed in KTS.

REQUIRED CLIMB RATE = CLIMB GRADIENT ÷ GS

Example:
- climb rate = 480 FPM, GS = 120 KTS
- 480 ÷ 120 = 4 %

Flight Manoeuvres & Cruise Flight

For Timed Turns divide the given number of degrees by 3 or
multiply them by 0.3.

TURN TIME (SEC) = DEGREES ÷ 3

TURN TIME (SEC) = DEGREES x 0.3

Example:
- number of degrees = 60 ÷ 3 = 20 SEC
- intended turn = 20° x 0.3 = 6 SEC

PILOT's BASICS

Optimizing Fuel Consumption:

> ✈ Increase Cruise Speed by 10% with a Headwind.
> ✈ Decrease Cruise Speed by 5% with a Tailwind.

The first 2 digits of a Course are equal to the sum of the Reciprocal Course and the 90-degree Course.

Example:
- ✈ runway 16/34: 1 + 6 = 7   respective 3 + 4 = 7
- ✈ XWind course = 250 = 2 + 5 = 7
- ✈ base course = 070 = 0 + 7 = 7

At a given Speed per Minute (NM/MIN) the number of degrees of the Pitch Change multiplied by 100 equals the Rate of Descent.

$$1° \text{ PITCH CHANGE} = 100 \text{ FPM} \times \text{NM/MIN}$$

Example:
- ✈ speed = 120 KTAS = 2 NM/MIN,
- ✈ 3° Pitch-Down

   Descent Rate = 2 x (3 x 100) = 600 FPM

or
- ✈ speed = 240 KTAS,
- ✈ 3° Pitch-Up
- ✈ 240 KTAS = 4 NM/MIN

  Climb Rate = 4 x 300 = 1200 FPM

Approach and Landing

- A Tailwind of 10% of the Landing Speed increases the <u>Landing Distance</u> by 20%.
- A Headwind of 10% of the Landing Speed decreases the <u>Landing Distance</u> by 20%.

10% TAILWIND = LANDING DISTANCE + 20%

10% HEADWIND = LANDING DISTANCE - 20%

The <u>Crosswind Component</u> is the Wind Speed multiplied by the Sine of the angle to the runway.

XWIND COMP = VW x SIN (RUNWAY ANGLE)

The Sine is 10% of the XWind angle + 2 and thereof 10%.

Example:
- angle = 20°
- 10% of 20 = 2 + 2 = 4, thereof 10% = 0.4

A 10% increase in the Landing Speed increases the <u>Stopping Distance</u> by 20%.

+10% LANDING SPEED = STOPPING DISTANCE +20%

The <u>Headwind/Tailwind Component</u> is the Wind Speed multiplied by the Cosine of the angle to the runway.

H-/T-WIND COMP = V_W x COS (RWY ANGLE)

The <u>Cosine of an Angle</u> equals the Sine of the difference between the actual angle to 90 degrees.

Example:
- angle = 20°, difference to 90° = 70°
- 10 % of 70 = 7 + 2 = 9, thereof 10 % = 0.9

PILOT's BASICS

A narrow runway appears to be longer; a wide runway appears to be shorter than actual length.

A slippery or wet runway may increase the Landing Distance by 50%.

The higher the Airport Elevation, the longer the Landing Distance.

An airport with a 1000 FT higher elevation increases the Stopping Distance by approximately 4%.

+1000 FT ELEVATION = STOPPING DISTANCE + 4%

Each KT over the correct Approach Speed V_{REF} moves the Touch Down Point 100 FT further down the runway.

A higher temperature increases the Stopping Distance because of the higher TAS. 10°C deviation from ISA increases Stopping Distance by approximately 5%.

+10°C ISA DEVIATION = STOPPING DISTANCE + 5%

PILOT's BASICS

CHAPTER 9

SUMMARY OF FORMULAE

Masses

MASSES – EXACT				
Mass	X	=	X	Mass
LBS	0.4536	KG	2.2045	LBS
KG	2.2045	LBS	0.4526	KG

MASSES – APPROXIMATION				
Mass	X	=	X	Mass
LBS	0.45	KG	2.2	LBS
KG	2.2	LBS	0.45	KG
(KG x 2) + 10 % = LBS			(LBS ÷ 2) – 10 % = KG	

Areas

AREAS – EXACT				
Area	X	=	X	Area
SQUARE FEET	0.0929	M^2	10.7639	SQUARE FEET

AREAS – APPROXIMATION				
Area	X	=	X	Area
SQUARE FEET	0.1	M^2	11	SQUARE FEET

PILOT's BASICS

Volumes

VOLUMES – EXACT				
Volume	X	=	X	Volume
LITRE	0.2641	USG	3.7853	LITRE
IMPG	1.201	USG	0.8326	IMPG
IMPG	4.546	LITRE	0.2199	IMPG

VOLUMES – APPROXIMATION				
Volume	X	=	X	Volume
LITRE	0.25	USG	3.8	LITRE
IMPG	1.2	USG	0.8	IMPG
IMPG	4.5	LITRE	0.2	IMPG

AVGAS – EXACT				
Volume	X	Weight	X	Volume
LITRE	0.719	KG	1.39	LITRE
USG	2.75	KG	0.3672	USG
IMPG	3.27		0.3058	IMPG
LITRE	1.58	LBS	0.631	LITRE
USG	6.0	LBS	0.167	USG
IMPG	7.18		0.1391	IMPG

AVGAS – APPROXIMATION				
Volume	X	Weight	X	Volume
LITRE	0.8	KG	1.5	LITRE
USG	2.8	KG	0.4	USG
IMPG	3.3		0.3	IMPG
LITRE	1.6	LBS	0.6	LITRE
USG	6.0	LBS	0.2	USG
IMPG	7.2		0.15	IMPG

PILOT's BASICS

JET-FUEL – EXACT (JET A1, 15° C)					
Volume	X	Weight	X	Volume
LITRE	0.796	KG	1.2565	LITRE
USG	3.085		0.3241	USG
IMPG	3,618		0.2764	IMPG
LITRE	1.7547	LBS	0.57	LITRE
USG	6.7		0.1506	USG
IMPG	7,977		0.1254	IMPG

JET-FUEL – APPROXIMATION				
Volume	X	Weight	X	Volume
LITRE	0.8	KG	1.25	LITRE
USG	3.8		0.3	USG
IMPG	4.6		0.3	IMPG
LITRE	1.8	LBS	0.6	LITRE
USG	6.7		0.15	USG
IMPG	8.0		0.15	IMPG

General Distances

EXACT		
SM	KM	NM
0.6213	1	0.5399
KM	NM	SM
1.852	1	1.1508
KM	SM	NM
1.6096	1	0.8689
M	KM	FT
1000	1	3208
M	NM	FT
1852	1	6076
M	SM	FT
1609	1	5280

APPROXIMATION
(KM ÷ 2) + 10% = NM
(NM x 2) – 10% = KM
(KM ÷ 2) + 20% = SM
(SM x 2) – 20% = KM
SM – 15% = NM
NM + 15% = SM
(FT ÷ 3) – 5% = M
(M x 3) + 5% = FT
FT ÷ 6000 = NM
NM x 6000 = FT
(FT ÷ 5000) – 5% = SM
(SM x 5000) + 5% = FT

PILOT's BASICS

Speeds

EXACT	
MPS*	FPM
1	196.85
5.08	1.000
MPS	KTS
1	1.9438
0.5145	1
MPS	KMH
1	3.6
0.277	1
KTS	KMH
1	1.852
0.5399	1

APPROXIMATION
MPS x 200 = FPM
FPM ÷ 200 = MPS
MPS x 2 = KTS
½ KTS = MPS
(MPS x 3) + 20% = KMH
(KMH ÷ 3) – 20% = MPS
(KTS x 2) - 10% = KMH
(KMH ÷ 2) + 10% = KTS

* MPS = Meter Per Second

RVR Values

EXACT		
FEET	METER	SM
6000	1870	1¼
5000	1600	1
4000	1250	3/4
2400	750	1/2
1600	500	1/4
800	250	1/8
400	125	

APPROXIMATION		
METER		FT
1850 x 3 +	300 =	6000
1600 x 3 +	250 =	5000
1250 x 3 +	200 =	4000
750 x 3 +	150 =	2400
500 x 3 +	100 =	1600
250 x 3 +	50 =	800
125 x 3 +	25 =	400

59

PILOT's BASICS

Time-Speed-Distance (TSD)

GROUND SPEED (KTS)	NM PER MINUTE (NM/MIN)
90	1.5
120	2.0
150	2.5
180	3.0
210	3.5
240	4.0
270	4.5
300	5.0
330	5.5
360	6.0
390	6.5
420	7.0
450	7.5
480	8.0
510	8.5

DISTANCE = GS x TIME

ETP-D = <u>Total Distance x Return Groundspeed (GS)</u>
Continue GS + Return GS

ETP-T = ETP-D ÷ Continue GS

PRN-D = END x   <u>GS x Return GS</u>
Continue GS + Return GS

END = Endurance

PNR-T = PNR-D ÷ Continue GS

PILOT's BASICS

Reciprocal Courses

COURSE <180°:
RECIPROCAL COURSE = COURSE + 200° – 20°

COURSE >180°:
RECIPROCAL COURSE = COURSE – 200° + 20°

```
COURSE =            0 0 0
                   +/– 2
                   –/+  2
RECIPROCAL COURSE =  X X X
```

The Rules:
✈ The first sign +/– is depending on the start course.
✈ The first result must not be negative; the first digit must not be greater than 3.
✈ The second calculation must use the opposite sign of the first calculation.
✈ The last digit always remains unchanged.

DME-Arc – Intercept: "1 in 60" Rule

DME DISTANCE	1° = NM
60	1
30	1/2 or 0.50
20	1/3 or 0.33
15	1/4 or 0.25
12	1/5 or 0.20
10	1/6 or 0.16

PILOT's BASICS

Turn Radius – "Lead Point" on a DME-Arc

TURN RADIUS (NM) = TAS ÷ 200

or

TURN RADIUS (NM) = (TAS x 1%) ÷ 2

TURN RADIUS (NM) = (MACH NUMBER x 10) – 2

Standard Rate Turn (SRT)

BANK ANGLE (BA) = (TAS ÷ 10) x 1.5

or

BANK ANGLE (BA) = (TAS + (TAS ÷ 2)) ÷ 10

or

BANK ANGLE (BA) = (TAS ÷ 10) + 7

Base Turn Angle (BT Angle)

BT ANGLE = $\dfrac{\text{FACTOR 36 (54)}}{\text{OUTBOUND TIME}}$

factor 36 up to 170 KTS
factor 54 above 170 KTS

OUTBOUND TIME = $\dfrac{\text{FACTOR 36 (54)}}{\text{BT ANGLE}}$

factor 36 up to 170 KTS
factor 54 above 170 KTS

Turns with the Magnetic Compass

UNOS – Undershoot North, Overshoot South

ANDS – Accelerate North, Decelerate South

"Lead-Point" in "magnetic" Turns

The turn is stopped on the magnetic compass heading from which the following value has been added or subtracted from the planned heading.

Latitude +/- 1/3 of the Bank Angle

✈ LEAD POINT =   ✈ TARGET COURSE +/- (LAT +/- 1/3 BANK ANGLE)

Descent

"3 in 1" Method   DISTANCE (NM) =   (ACTUAL FL – PLANNED FL) ÷ 10 x 3 + 10   +   +/- 2 NM for each 10 KTS Head- or Tailwind

Or

DISTANCE (NM) =   (ACTUAL FL – PLANNED FL) ÷ 3 + 10   +   +/- 2 NM for each 10 KTS Head- or Tailwind

PILOT's BASICS

Minimum Climb Gradient

| % x GS = ROC/ROD in FPM |

or

| FT/NM x (GS ÷ 60) |

Correcting Altitude Deviations

| ROD/ROC (FPM) = DEVIATION x 2 |

| ROD/ROC = Rate of Descent/Climb in FPM |

Initiation of the Level-Off

| ROD/ROC within 1000 FT = ALTITUDE TO GO |

Crosswind (XWind)

WIND ANGLE TO THE RWY	FACTOR	XWIND FACTOR	XWIND COMPONENT
000°	0.0	0%	nothing
030°	0.5	50%	half
045°	0.7	70%	2/3
060°	0.9	90%	nearly full
090°	1.0	100%	full

Drift Corrections

| DRIFT CORRECTION = (XWIND COMPONENT x 60) ÷ TAS |

| DRIFT CORRECTION = XWIND COMPONENT ÷ Y |

(Y = NM/MIN)

| DRIFT CORRECTION = (WIND ANGLE x WIND SPEED) ÷ TAS |

PILOT's BASICS

When flying Mach-Numbers

> 1° DRIFT CORRECTION = XWIND COMPONENT ÷ (M x 10)

Course Corrections

> BANK = HEADING TO GO

VDP – DME – Method

> VDP (DME) = HAT ÷ 300
>
> HAT = Height above Threshold

VDP – Timing – Method

> VDP (SEC) = HAT ÷ 10

Descent Rate

> ROD (FPM) = GS x 5
> (+ 200 FPM for Non-Precision Approaches)

True Airspeed (TAS)

> KTAS = KIAS + ((KIAS x (ALT in 1000's)) x 2%)

> TAS = IAS + Z%
>
> Z% = 2 x ALT (in 1000 FT)

PILOT's BASICS

Temperatures

$$°F = (2 \times °C) + 30$$
$$°C = (°F - 30) \div 2$$

$$°F = (2 \times °C) - 10\% + 32$$
$$°C = ((°F - 32) + 10\%) \div 2$$

or

$$°F = (9/5 \times °C) + 32$$
$$°C = (°F - 32) \times 5/9$$

Standard Temperature

$$\text{ISA STD TEMPERATURE (°C)} = 15 - (FL \div 10 \times 2)$$

Cloud Base

$$\text{CLOUD BASE} = \text{SPREAD (°C)} \times 2.5$$

or

$$\text{CLOUD BASE} = \text{SPREAD (°C)} \times 400$$

Fuel Dumping

$$\text{DUMP TIME} = \text{AMOUNT OF FUEL} \div \text{DUMP RATE}$$

$$\text{AMOUNT OF FUEL} = \text{DUMP RATE} \times \text{TIME}$$

Aquaplaning/Hydroplaning Speed

$$V_{HP} \text{ (KTS)} = 9 \times \sqrt{\text{TYRE PRESSURE (PSI)}}$$

PILOT's BASICS

Time in Decimals

MIN/SEC	DECIMAL
3	0.05
6	0.10
9	0.15
12	0.20
15	0.25
18	0.30
21	0.35
24	0.40
27	0.45
30	0.50

MIN/SEC	DECIMAL
33	0.55
36	0.60
39	0.65
42	0.70
45	0.75
48	0.80
51	0.85
54	0.90
57	0.95
60	1.00

Addition of Times

TIME		INPUT INTO THE CALCULATOR
4:56	=	4056
2:18	=	+ 2018
1:55	=	+ 1055
5:20	=	+ 5020 =
14:29		12149 third last digit is not 0 →
		+ 940 =
		13089 the 2 last digits are above 59 →
		+ 940 =
		14029 → 14:29 H

67

PILOT's BASICS

Subtraction of Times

TIME		INPUT INTO THE CALCULATOR
14:07	=	14007
- 4:56	=	- 4056
- 2:18	=	- 2018
- 1:55	=	- 1055 =
4:58		6878 third last digit is not 0 →
		- 940 =
		5938 third last digit is not 0 →
		- 940 =
		4998 third last digit is not 0 →
		-940 =
		4058 → 4:58 H

Mixed Calculation

TIME		INPUT INTO THE CALCULATOR
14:07	=	14007
- 4:56	=	- 4056
9:11	=	9951 third last digit is not 0 →
		- 940 =
		9011 (= 9:11 H)
+1:55		+ 1055 =
11:06	=	10066 the 2 last digits are above 59 →
		+ 940 =
		11006 → 11:06 H

68

PILOT's BASICS

CHAPTER 10

ABBREVATIONS

AGL	Above Ground Level
ATC	Air Traffic Control
ATIS	Automatic Terminal Information Service
C	Celsius, Centigrade
DME	Distance Measuring Equipment
ETE	Estimated Time Enroute
ETA	Estimated Time of Arrival
F	Fahrenheit
FAF	Final Approach Fix
FL	Flight Level
FPM	Feet Per Minute
FT	Feet
GAL	Gallons
GS	Ground Speed
GS	Glide Slope
HAT	Height Above Threshold
HW	Headwind
IAS	Indicated Airspeed
IFR	Instrument Flight Rules
ILS	Instrument Landing System
IN	Inches
ISA	International Standard Atmosphere
KTS	Knots (Nautical Miles Per Hour)
KM	Kilometre
KMH	Kilometres Per Hour
KPH	Kilometres Per Hour
LBS	Pounds
LOC	Localizer

PILOT's BASICS

M	Mach Number
M	Meters
MB	Millibars
MDA	Minimum Descent Altitude
METAR	Aviation Routine Weather Report
MIN	Minute
MPH	Miles Per Hour
MPS	Meters Per Second
MSL	Mean Sea Level
NM	Nautical Mile
NDB	Non Directional Beacon
NOTAM	Notices To Airmen
PDP	Planned Descent Point
PIREP	Pilots Report
PPM	Pounds Per Minute
PSI	Pounds per Square Inch
RVR	Runway Visual Range
S	Second
SL	Sea Level
SM	Statue Mile
SRT	Standard Rate Turn
TAF	Terminal Aerodrome Forecast
TAS	True Airspeed
TOD	Top Of Descent
TW	Tailwind
V	Velocity
VDP	Visual Descent Point
VFR	Visual Flight Rules
VHF	Very High Frequency
VHP	Hydroplaning Speed
VAR	Variation
VOR	VHF Omnidirectional Range

PILOT's BASICS

CHAPTER 11

TABLES

Standard Weights

TYPE	KG	LBS
1 LITRE Jet A	0.8	1.80
1 GAL Jet A	3.06	6.75
1 LITRE AVGAS	0.72	1.60
1 GAL AVGAS	2.72	6.00
1 LITRE OIL	0.9	1.98
1 QUART OIL	0.85	1.875
1 GAL OIL	3.4	7.50

ICAO – Standard Atmosphere

PRESSURE	1013 MB/HP=760MM Hg=14.7 PSI
TEMPERATURE	15°C = 59°F
SPEED OF SOUND	741.4 NM/HR = 1087.4 FT/SEC

MPS	FPM	MPS	FPM	MPS	FPM	MPS	FPM
1	197	6	1.181	11	2.165	16	3.150
1.5	295	6.5	1.279	11.5	2.263	16.5	3.248
2	394	7	1.378	12	2.362	17	3.346
2.5	492	7.5	1.476	12.5	2.460	17.5	3.444
3	591	8	1.575	13	2.559	18	3.543
3.5	689	8.5	1.673	13.5	2.657	18.5	3.641
4	787	9	1.772	14	2.756	19	3.740
4.5	885	9.5	1.870	14.5	2.854	19.5	3.838
5	984	10	1.969	15	2.953	20	3.937
5.5	1.082	10.5	2.067	15.5	3.051		

PILOT's BASICS

Exact Conversions

1 MB/HP	=	0.02953 INCH HG
1 INCHHG	=	33.863 M/HP
1 METER/SEC	=	196.85 FT/MIN
1 METER/SEC	=	1.9438 NM/HR
1 NM/HR	=	101.2 FT/MIN = 1.68 FT/SEC
1 SM/HR	=	88 FT/MIN = 1.46 FT/SEC
1 KG	=	2.2046 LBS
1 LBS	=	0.45359 kg
1 KM	=	0.53996 NM
1 KM	=	0.62137 SM
1 NM	=	6076 FT
1 NM	=	1.852 KM = 1.15 SM
1 FT	=	0.3048 M
1 M	=	3.2909 FT = 1.0936 YARDS
1 YARD	=	0.9144 M
1 INCH	=	25.4 MM
1 SQUARE INCH	=	6.5 CM^2
1 CUBIC INCH	=	16 CM^3
1 LITRE	=	0.26418 USG
1 KHZ	=	1.000 HZ
1 MHZ	=	1.000 KHZ = 1.000.000 HZ

PILOT's BASICS

FRACTION	DECIMAL	FRACTION	DECIMAL
1/1	1.000	1/7	0.143
1/2	0.500	1/8	0.125
1/3	0.333	1/9	0.111
1/4	0.250	1/10	0.100
1/5	0.200	1/11	0.091
1/6	0.167	1/12	0.083

SQUARE	NUMBER	ROOT	SQUARE	NUMBER	ROOT
1	1	1	81	9	3
4	2	1.41	100	10	3.16
9	3	1.73	121	11	3.32
16	4	2	144	12	3.46
25	5	2.24	169	13	3.61
36	6	2.45	196	14	3.74
49	7	2.65	225	15	3.87
64	8	2.83	256	16	4

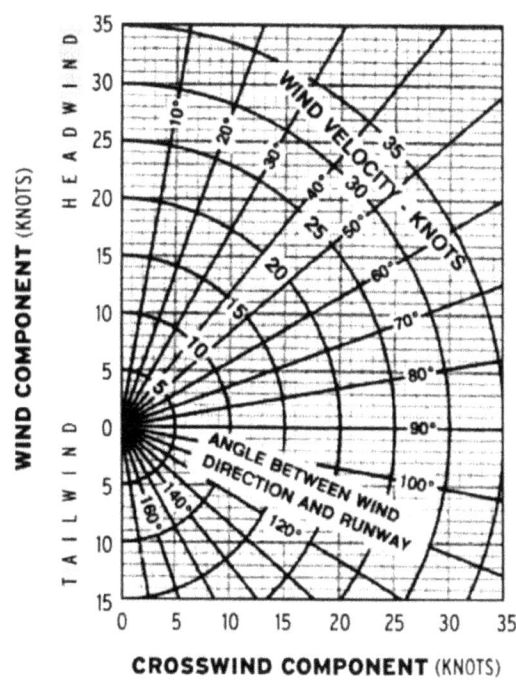

PILOT's BASICS

TEMPERATURES

°C	°F	°C	°F	°C	°F	°C	°F
-29	-20.2	-14	6.8	1	33.8	16	60.8
-28	-18.4	-13	8.6	2	35.6	17	62.6
-27	-16.6	-12	10.4	3	37.6	18	64.4
-26	-14.8	-11	12.2	4	39.2	19	66.2
-25	-13.0	-10	14.0	5	41.0	20	68.0
-24	-11.2	-9	15.8	6	42.8	21	69.8
-23	-9.4	-8	17.6	7	44.6	22	71.6
-22	-7.6	-7	19.4	8	46.4	23	73.4
-21	-5.8	-6	21.2	9	48.2	24	75.2
-20	-4.0	-5	23.0	10	50.0	25	77.0
-19	-2.2	-4	24.8	11	51.8	26	78.8
-18	-0.4	-3	26.6	12	53.6	27	80.6
-17	1.4	-2	28.4	13	55.4	28	82.4
-16	3.2	-1	30.2	14	57.2	29	84.2
-15	5.0	0	32.0	15	59.0	30	86.0

WIND-ANGLE	10	20	30	40	50	60	70	80
WIND-SPEED	\multicolumn{8}{c}{CROSSWIND COMPONENT}							
5	1	2	3	3	4	4	5	5
10	2	3	5	6	8	9	9	10
15	3	5	8	10	11	13	14	15
20	3	7	10	13	15	17	19	20
25	4	9	13	16	19	22	23	25
30	5	10	15	19	23	26	28	29
35	6	12	18	22	27	30	33	34
40	7	14	20	26	31	35	38	39
45	8	15	23	29	34	39	42	44
50	9	17	25	32	38	43	47	49

PILOT's BASICS

ALTITUDE (FT)	STD TEMP (°C)	ALTITUDE (FT)	STD TEMP (°C)
SL	+15	21.000	-27
3.000	+9	23.000	-31
5.000	+5	25.000	-35
7.000	+1	27.000	-38
9.000	-1	29.000	-42
11.000	-7	31.000	-46
13.000	-11	33.000	-50
15.000	-15	35.000	-54
17.000	-19	37.000	-57
19.000	-23		

DISTANCES M – FT – IN – MM						
METER	M/FT	FEET	INCH	IN/MM	MILLI-METER	
0.3048	1	3.2808	0.03937	1	25.4
0.609	2	6.561	0.787	2	50.8
0.914	3	10.763	0.118	3	76.2
1.219	4	14.351	0.157	4	101.6
1.524	5	16.404	0.196	5	127.0
1.888	6	19.684	0.236	6	152.4
2.133	7	22.965	0.275	7	177.8
2.438	8	26.246	0.314	8	203.2
2.743	9	29.527	0.354	9	228.6
3.048	10	32.808	0.393	10	254.0
6.096	20	65.616	0.787	20	508.0
9.144	30	107.636	1.181	30	762.0
12.192	40	143.515	1.574	40	1016.0
15.240	50	164.04	1.968	50	1270.0
18.880	60	196.848	2.362	60	1524.0
21.330	70	229.656	2.755	70	1778.0
24.384	80	262.464	3.149	80	2032.0
27.432	90	295.272	3.543	90	2286.0
30.48	100	328.0	3.937	100	2540.0

PILOT's BASICS

SM	KM	NM		KM	SM	NM
0.62137	1	0.53996		1.6093	1	0.86898
1.24	2	1.08		3.22	2	1.74
1.86	3	1.62		4.83	3	2.61
2.49	4	2.16		6.44	4	3.48
3.11	5	2.70		8.05	5	4.34
3.73	6	3.24		9.66	6	5.21
4.35	7	3.78		11.27	7	6.08
4.97	8	4.32		12.87	8	6.95
5.59	9	4.86		14.48	9	7.82
6.21	10	5.40		16.09	10	8.69
12.43	20	10.80		32.19	20	17.38
18.64	30	16.20		48.28	30	26.07
24.85	40	21.60		64.37	40	34.76
31.07	50	27.00		80.47	50	43.45
37.28	60	32.40		96.56	60	52.14
43.50	70	37.80		112.65	70	60.83

KM	NM	SM
1.8520	1	1.1508
3.70	2	2.30
5.56	3	3.45
7.41	4	4.60
9.26	5	5.75
11.11	6	6.90
12.96	7	8.06
14.82	8	9.21
16.67	9	10.36
18.52	10	11.51
37.04	20	23.02
55.56	30	34.52
74.08	40	46.03
92.60	50	57.54
111.12	60	69.05
129.64	70	80.56

PILOT's BASICS

WEIGHT			VOLUME		
LBS	KG/LBS	KG	USGAL	L/USG	LITRE
2.2046	1	0.45359	0.26418	1	3.7853
4.4092	2	0.9072	0.5283	2	7.5706
6.6138	3	1.3607	0.7925	3	14.3284
8.8184	4	1.8143	1.0567	4	15.1412
11.022	5	2.2679	1.3209	5	18.9265
13.227	6	2.7215	1.5850	6	22.7118
15.432	7	3.1751	1.8492	7	26.4971
17.636	8	3.6287	2.1134	8	30.2824
19.841	9	4.0823	2.3776	9	34.0677
22.046	10	4.535	2.642	10	37.853
44.092	20	9.072	5.283	20	75.706
66.138	30	13.607	7.925	30	143.284
88.184	40	18.143	10.567	40	151.412
110.22	50	22.679	13.209	50	189.265
132.27	60	27.215	15.850	60	227.118
154.32	70	31.751	18.492	70	264.971
176.36	80	36.287	21.134	80	302.824
198.41	90	40.823	23.776	90	340.677
220.46	100	45.35	26.42	100	378.53

PILOT's BASICS

CHAPTER 12

TRAINING EXAMPLES

HYDROPLANING	
TYRE PRESSURE (PSI)	V_{HP}
50	?
120	?
150	?
230	?

CONVERSION OF TEMPERATURES				
°C	METHOD 1	METHOD 2	METHOD 3	°F
12	?	?	?	?
25	?	?	?	?
0	?	?	?	?
?	?	?	?	40
?	?	?	?	72

STANDARD TEMPERATURE/DEVIATION			
ALTITUDE	ISA	ACTUAL TEMP	TEMP DEV
5.000	?	+ 20° C	?
8.000	?	+ 15° C	?
FL 210	?	- 10° C	?
FL 350	?	- 60° C	?

WIND ANGLE	WIND SPEED	XWIND
030	20	?
050	20	?
070	18	?

PILOT's BASICS

TAS	XWIND	DRIFT
150 KTAS	12 KTS	?
360 KTAS	48 KTS	?
90 KTAS	30 KTS	?
0.78 M	50 KTS	?

GIVEN	CONVERT TO
200 KTS	? MPH
180 MPH	? KTS
8 MPS	? KTS
9 KM	? SM
55 USG AVGAS	? LBS
1.000 LBS AVGAS	? USG
500 USG JETA1	? LBS
8.500 LBS JETA1	? USG

DUMP RATE	TIME	FUEL DUMPED
1.300	?	6.500
2.500	?	45.000
2.500	?	30.000
2.200	?	11.000?
1.500	7:00	?
1.200	11:00	?
?	5:00	12.500
?	16:00	48.000
2.000	?	20.000

BANK ANGLE	START HEADING	TARGET HEADING	LATITUDE	LEAD POINT
15 R	270	360	45 N	?
15 L	270	180	34 N	?
25 R	360	090	40 N	?
20 R	090	190	40 N	?
15 R	270	360	30 N	?
25 R	090	190	40 N	?

PILOT's BASICS

DME-ARC	SPEED	START RADIAL	END RADIAL	LEAD RADIAL (STD RATE)
15	200	047	011	?
20	200	047	011	?
12	200	047	011	?

KTAS/M	STD RATE TURN BANK ANGLE	TURN RADIUS (SRT/30° MAX BANK)
90	?°	? NM
120	?°	? NM
200	?°	? NM
0.80	30° DEG	? NM

KIAS	ALTITUDE	KTAS
100	10.000	?
140	5.000	?
200	13.000	?
280	FL 350	?

KTAS	WIND (KTS)	TIME (MIN)	DISTANCE (NM)
240	60 TW	?	200
280	70 HW	10:00	?
150	0	?	5
?	0	4:00	20
420	60 TW	?	400
?	0	2:00	14
?	0	90:00	600
500	0	45:00	?
?	0	40:00	340

PILOT's BASICS

TRAINING EXAMPLES – RESULTS

TYRE PRESSURE (PSI)	V_{HP} (KTS)
50	63
120	99
150	108
230	135

°C	METHOD 1	METHOD 2	METHOD 3	°F
12	54	54	54	?
25	75	77	80	?
0	30	32	30	?
?	5	4	5	40
?	21	22	21	72

WINDANGLE	WINDSPEED	XWIND
030	20	10
050	20	14
070	18	16

TAS	XWIND	DRIFT
150 KTAS	12 KTS	5°
360 KTAS	48 KTS	8°
90 KTAS	30 KTS	20°
0.78 M	50 KTS	7°

ALTITUDE	ISA	ACTUAL TEMP	TEMP DEV
5.000	5°	+ 20° C	+15°
8.000	-1°	+ 15° C	+16°
FL 210	-27°	- 10° C	+17°
FL 350	-55°	- 60° C	-5°

PILOT's BASICS

GIVEN	CONVERTED TO
200 KTS	230 MPH
180 MPH	156 KTS
8 MPS	16 KTS
9 KM	6 SM
55 USG AVGAS	330 LBS
1.000 LBS AVGAS	167 USG
500 USG JETA1	3.350 LBS
5.000 LBS JETA1	750 USG
8.500 LBS JETA1	1.275 USG

DUMP RATE	TIME	FUEL DUMPED
1.300	5:00	6.500
2.500	18:00	45.000
2.500	12:00	30.000
2.200	5:00	11.000
1.500	7:00	10.500
1.200	11:00	13.200
2.500	5:00	12.500
3.000	16:00	48.000
2.000	10:00	20.000

DME-ARC	SPEED	START RADIAL	END RADIAL	LEAD RADIAL (STD RATE)
15	200	047	011	4
20	200	047	011	3
12	200	047	011	5

BANK ANGLE	START HEADING	TARGET HEADING	LATITUDE	LEAD POINT
15 R	270	360	45 N	310
15 L	270	180	34 N	151
25 R	360	090	40 N	082
20 R	090	190	40 N	223

PILOT's BASICS

KTAS/M	STD RATE TURN BANK ANGLE	TURN RADIUS (SRT/30° MAX BANK)
90	13.5°	0.5 NM
120	18°	0.6 NM
200	30°	1 NM
0.80	30°	6 NM

KIAS	ALTITUDE (FT)	KTAS
100	10.000	120
140	5.000	154
200	13.000	252
280	FL350	476

KTAS	WIND (KTS)	TIME (MIN)	DISTANCE (NM)
240	60 TW	40:00	200
280	70 HW	10:00	35
150	0	2:00	5
300	0	4:00	20
420	60 TW	50:00	400
420	0	2:00	14
400	0	90:00	600
500	0	45:00	375
510	0	40:00	340

PILOT's BASICS

CHAPTER 13

CHECKLIST „MNEMONICS"

Unfortunately not everybody is using the complete checklists as required.

To assure that at least the most important things are completed here are some Mnemonics checklists.

Mnemonics are key words which can easily be remembered and should trigger the basic items of a checklist.

Before Take-Off Checklists

C	Controls	Free, full travel & correct
I	Instruments	Engine- & flight instruments, altimeter
G	Gasoline	Fuel-Selector, Fuel-Pump
A	Attitude	Flaps and Trim set
R	Runup	Engine run-up, magneto check

C	Controls	Free, full travel and correct
I	Instruments	Engine- & flight instruments, altimeter
G	Gasoline	Fuel-Selector, Fuel-Pump
A	Attitude	Flaps & Trim set
R	Radios	COM & NAV frequencies set for departure
E	Emergency	Briefing
S	Safety	Doors closed & locked, Seatbelts & Shoulder harnesses on

B	Boost	Pump ON
L	Lights	ON as required
I	Instruments	Set
T	Transponder	ON
T	Takeoff	Time recorded
S	Seat Belts	Secured

PILOT's BASICS

Level Off

P	Pitch	level off at cruising altitude/flight level
T	Power	set cruise power
T	Trim	trim the aircraft

Instrument Approach, Holding

6T	Turn	to proper heading
T	Time	to hold or approach (or navigation leg for VFR)
T	Tune or Twist	the OBS to the appropriate course
T	Transition, or Throttle	to the proper configuration & airspeed for power reduction
T	Talk	to air traffic control
T	Test	the directional gyro by comparing it to the compass

Nearing the Destination Airport

W	Weather	ATIS, ASOS, AWOS, etc.
I	Instruments	set, particulary the Altimeter
R	Radios	tuned and identified
E	Elevation	altitude for the Final Approach Fix
T	Trimming	to the missed approach point
A	Altitudes	Descision Height/Minimum Descent Altitude
P	Procedure	for the missed approach

Position Report

A	Aircraft	identification
P	Position	name of the fix
T	Time	crossing the fix
A	Altitude	
T	Type	of flight plan, VFR or IFR
E	Estimated	time of arrival at the next reporting point
N	Name	of the next reporting point

85

Mandatory Items to be Reported under IFR

H	Holding	time & altitude entering and leaving
A	Altitude changes	VFR on top & leaving assigned altitudes
M	Missed approach	when executing
S	Safety of flight	anything that affects it
A	Airspeed changes	of 5% or 10 knots
C	Communication	or navigation capability loss
C	Climb rate	when unable to maintain a 500 ft/min climb

Before Landing Checklists

G	Gasoline	Fuel-Selector, Fuel-Pump
U	Undercarriage	Check down & locked
M	Mixture	Rich
S	Switches	Landing light, NAV lights, Pitot Heat
S	Safety	Seatbelts & Shoulder harnesses, passenger briefing

G	Gasoline	Fuel-Selector, Fuel-Pump
U	Undercarriage	Check down & locked
M	Mixture	Rich
P	Propeller	High RPM
S	Switches	Landing light, NAV lights, Pitot Heat
S	Safety	Seatbelts & Shoulder harnesses, passenger briefing

B	Breaks	Test
U	Undercarriage	Check down & locked
M	Mixture	Rich
P	Propeller	High RPM
F	Flaps	Landing configuration
I	Instruments	Directional Gyro, Compass
C	Carburator Heat	Check
H	Hatches & Harness	Secure

PILOT's BASICS

Final Approach

M	Mixture	Set
P	Propeller	High RPM
G	Green	on landing gear indicator

Shut Down Checklist

R	Radios	All radios OFF
E	Electrical	All electrics OFF
M	Mixture	Idle cut-off
M	Master Switch	OFF
M	Magnetos	OFF

S	Switches	All electrics OFF
L	Lean	Mixture idle cut-off
I	Ignition	Magnetos OFF
M	Master Switch	OFF

5M	Music	COM- & NAV-Radios OFF
M	Magnetos	Verify short-circuit is functional
M	Mixture	Lean
M	Magnetos	OFF
M	Master Switch	OFF

Securing the Aircraft

M	Master	Master Switch OFF
I	Ignition	Ignition/Magneto switch OFF
D	Doors	Doors & Windows latched
G	Gust	Gust Lock installed
E	ELT	Emergency Locator Transmitter OFF
T	Tiedowns	Tiedowns secured

PILOT's BASICS

Emergencies

A	Airspeed	Best Glide
B	Best field	Pick landing site
C	Checklist	Restart, fire, etc.
D	Declare emergency	Squawk 7700
E	Execute emergency landing	Fuel OFF, doors open, etc.

Oxygen Systems

P	Pressure
R	Regulator
I	Indicator
C	Connector
E	Emergencies

www.ingramcontent.com/pod-product-compliance
Lightning Source LLC
Chambersburg PA
CBHW050703160426
43194CB00010B/1987

FACT-O-PEDIA

WHALES, DOLPHINS AND OTHER SEA CREATURES

MOONSTONE

Published in Moonstone
by Rupa Publications India Pvt. Ltd 2023
7/16, Ansari Road, Daryaganj
New Delhi 110002

Sales centres:
Prayagraj Bengaluru Chennai
Hyderabad Jaipur Kathmandu
Kolkata Mumbai

Copyright © Rupa Publications India Pvt. Ltd 2023

All rights reserved.
No part of this publication may be reproduced, transmitted,
or stored in a retrieval system, in any form or by any means,
electronic, mechanical, photocopying, recording or otherwise,
without the prior permission of the publisher.

P-ISBN: 978-93-5702-299-6
E-ISBN: 978-93-5702-284-2

First impression 2023

10 9 8 7 6 5 4 3 2 1

This book is sold subject to the condition that it shall not,
by way of trade or otherwise, be lent, resold, hired out, or otherwise
circulated, without the publisher's prior consent, in any form of binding
or cover other than that in which it is published.